TULLYS

ISBN: 978-1-943488-05-6

Published by: Editorial ILUMINA S.A. de C.V.

Printed in Mexico
By Offset Santiago S.A. de C.V.
Río San Joaquín 436, Col. Ampliación Granada
CP 11520, México D.F.

Brainy Shu in: A happy mind
First edition: June 2016

Layout and editorial design: Paola Alonso.
Conceptual Art: Rosa Maria Campos Cruz.
Editorial review: Shaula Vega. Jonathan Venguer.

Brainy Shu in:
A HAPPY MIND

Text and illustrations by BIBIANA DOMIT

Hi, my name is Shu.
I am a very intelligent and extremely punctual girl.
I love reading, going to school
and doing my homework.

My friends call me Brainy Shu.
They say I know everything!
Maybe it's because
I have read more than 9,999 books.

The place I love the most is my science lab!
That's where I spend most of my time
mixing potions and doing experiments.

One day I discovered one of the best
formulas to solve the problems in our lives!
Here's how it happened:

It was Tuesday at 6:48 am.
I was in my science lab mixing
cromausigos verdiuximos liquid with frantosphordi
powder and gengibreum moloteun extract.

I looked at the clock and realized it was time for school. I grabbed my backpack and quickly head out.

As I took my twelfth step, I heard a terrible noise!
BBBRRRRROOOOAAAAAAAAMMMMMMMM!

In terror I screamed: "Aaaahhh! What in the world
was that?!". I ran and hid behind some bushes.

The loud noise continued.
BBBRRRRROOOOAAAAAAAAMMMMMMMMM!

I was really scared! I imagined it could be a big monster or aliens landing on planet earth.

Or even worse!
A Tyrannosaurus
Carnivorous Rex that
wanted to eat me!!!

BBBRRRRROOOOAAAAAAAAMMMMMMMMM!
The noise continued.
I tried moving my body to walk to school,
but I couldn't.
I was paralyzed in fear!

HAPPY THOUGHTS MAKE YOU STRONG!

Right when I was about to faint,
I opened my eyes and realized that it was my
thoughts that were making me scared.

I took a deep breath and remembered
what my grandpa used to tell me:
"If you ever feel lonely, sad or afraid.
Just think happy thoughts!
You'll see fear go away."

That was the perfect
moment to try my grandpa's formula.
I closed my eyes but I couldn't think
of anything.

Without loosing faith I tried again.
I closed my eyes and waited a bit more.
Suddenly, there it was! A happy thought came to mind!

Followed by more happy thoughts:
My best friends, cookies,
rainy days, my camera.

BBBRRRRROOOOAAAAAAAAAMMMMMMMMM!
I heard the noise again.
This time I was feeling good and strong!

In my mind there was no more
room for scary ideas.

My head was filled with
more and more happy thoughts!
My science lab, flamenco dance,
my hot tub, tea time.

With every happy thought I felt stronger.

I continued to walk and the noise got even louder.
But I was not afraid anymore!

My grandpa's formula worked!
And I could use it any time.
I just had to think of happy thoughts and
that gave me strength to go on.

A little further up the road, I realized that the strange noise was not a monster. It was just a big construction truck!

HAPPY THOUGHTS MAKE YOU STRONG!

I made it to school on time and told my friends about my new formula:

"HAPPY THOUGHTS MAKE YOU STRONG"

If one day you feel scared, worried or sad, remember the good and happy times you've had!

You'll see a smile appear on your face, making you feel good and clearing all trouble away!

TULLYS

Brainy Shu

This english girl is so smart, her friends call her "living encyclopedia".
She is always tidy and perfectly on time.
Shu lives with her grandparents, and spends most of the day in her science lab making experiments and new discoveries.

Messy Mo in:
THE BIG TRUTH
Learning the Value of HONESTY
Text and illustrations by: BIBIANA DOMIT

Nina Noodles in:
GOOD THINGS TAKE TIME
Learning the value of PATIENCE
Text and illustrations by: BIBIANA DOMIT

Silent Silus in:
LUCKY ME!
Learning the Value of CONFIDENCE
Text and illustrations by: BIBIANA DOMIT

Princess B in:
LIFE IS A ROLLER COASTER
Learning the Value of CHOICE
Text and illustrations by: BIBIANA DOMIT

Pete the Poet in:
I AM UNIQUE!
Learning the Value of UNIQUENESS
Text and illustrations by: BIBIANA DOMIT

Brainy Shu in:
A HAPPY MIND
Learning the Value of POSITIVE THINKING
Text and illustrations by: BIBIANA DOMIT

www.tullys.tv